You Were Made for Better:

A Writing Study for the Incarcerated

by L.A. Ridley

ISBN: 979-8-89589-879-6

Overview

You Were Made for Better is a 10-week writing self-study designed to help those incarcerated or newly released from a correctional facility discover a new way of reflection through writing. Through weekly prompts, writers can analyze their own actions and decisions and hopefully visualize new ways of living as they move forward in their life journeys. Most of all, it is hoped that they will realize how even though they have made mistakes, they do not have to allow those mistakes to define them. There is a better way, and they have the choice to explore that road and become a better version of themselves.

Lesson Outline

This self-study is dedicated to DL, AC, and CG,
who fight the good fight daily in hopes of finding their better.

The nightmare clings to the crevices of your mind as you open your eyes. Your bunkmate above you is shifting aimlessly in his bed, the sounds of his restless shuffling echoing throughout your small closet-sized cell. You are drenched in sweat, both because it is hot in your cell and because your body is reacting to the nightmare that sent your heart racing, awakening you with a start. You glance over at the two other people who share your cell. One is sleeping; the other is staring aimlessly at the ceiling above, eyes reflecting emptiness. The guards will arrive to initiate count, and you may or may not be fortunate enough to go and eat in the prison cafeteria; such will depend on whether the pod where you are housed is free of violence during this particular week. There will be no early-morning treks to your kitchen to eat breakfast or brew coffee, no afternoon trips to restaurants with friends, and no evening outings with family members. This is your life, 365 days a year, for the foreseeable future. While you may realize that you deserve this fate, it does not make this day-to-day vacuum of hopelessness or despair any easier to bear. You are an incarcerated prisoner, serving time for bad decisions, un-retractable mistakes, painful violence, or a combination of all of these. Without hope of a better life on the outside, this situation is the reality for the more than two million people currently serving time behind bars in the United States. For most of you, every day is a struggle to survive, not just physically, but also emotionally and mentally.

Although statistics vary, studies show that more than 50 percent of those of you who are incarcerated will return to prison within two to three years of being released. Other figures put that number closer to 90 percent if you change nothing during your time of incarceration.

Many of you have landed in prison because of circumstances in your youth that led to broken homes, poverty, violence, and little to no education. Some of you were deprived of stable homes where the basic necessities were not provided, let alone an education or the the basic emotional needs of love and support. While no one cannot condone these acts that many of you have committed, and I feel for the families of your victims, I wonder what would have happened if you had been given many of the same benefits in life that I received growing up.

To be clear, I am not excusing your behavior; however, I realize that you are well aware of the impact of your mistakes. You alone have to deal with the weight of these crimes on daily, and you are clearly paying for these crimes in painful ways that most people will never know.

However, while I may never excuse what you did, I have grown to understand how and why most offenders do what they do. I have learned through my own learning process that, as a fellow human, you are worthy of dignity. Your life has meaning, and I believe that someone out there cares about you—even if you don't care about yourself. It is for this reason that I created this study and hope you find meaning throughout this writing journey.

If you have decided that there is no hope and there is no use trying to become a good or better person, then this study is not for you. If you don't care about anyone but yourself or have no desire to change your course, this study is not for you. If it is easier to take drugs and waste your life in a state of mental incapacitation, this study is not for you. If you would rather spend your life in a room by yourself because you hate people that much, this study is not for you. If you embrace your criminality and don't care about changing it, this course is not for you.

If, however, you are seeking ways to discover the better version of yourself, to find meaning and/or purpose in what you are going through, then this course might be the beginning of a new journey for you. At the minimum, it might give you a new perspective. Some people may say that I am idealistic or naive, but I look for the good in every human, and I have no regrets in living life in this manner. I care what happens to people—not just the people in my own life, but the people I do not know as well.

I know that the environment in which you currently find yourself is merciless. I do not pretend to know what you experience every day. I also must concede that some of the ideas I propose may be foreign to you, some seemingly downright impossible. Maybe you are correct. I acknowledge that it is easy for me to give advice from a place of freedom and autonomy over my own life. However, I think that we have to start somewhere in implementing change, and even little changes can go a long way. I know that I would likely not survive a day in your shoes. I commend those of you who are seeking to discover a hope for something different—a better life, even behind the walls. I hope this can help.

So Why a Writing Course for Felons?

When one looks up the definition of the verb, *write*, many alternate verbs are used: communicate, form words, express, execute, compose, among others. All of these verbs involve the act of sitting down with pen and paper or at a computer and putting into print, recording, what we are thinking in our minds. While a simple process externally, it is quite a complicated process internally: one that can be easily completed by some, but can be a monstrous struggle for others.

Before you begin any writing venture, whether a journal, email, letter, post, poem, short story, application for a job, or even on a grand scale, a novel, you must first consider both our purpose and our audience for writing. There are various purposes for writing. In general, when you write something that is to be shared with others, you write to inform, you write to persuade, you write to entertain, and you write to inspire. I can also throw in another one that permeates this society: we write to incite negativity or anger—something we have seen in this present day more than in years past. If, on the other hand, you are writing just for yourself, writing can take on other purposes: you can write to process, you can write to cope, you can write to grieve, and you can write to record—your past, your present, and your aspirations for the future.

When you are writing for yourself, you are writing to try to sort through what is happening in your life, to make sense of it, to communicate with your deity, or to deal with the pain or joy you may be experiencing. In doing so, the act becomes very much an internal act, in addition to being an external act. While the other purposes of writing call for external audiences, when you are writing to process, you are writing for an audience of one: YOU.

I firmly believe writing has the ability to heal in ways nothing else can. It allows you to be real with yourself. It allows you to express what you are feeling. It allows you to organize your thoughts and process them more effectively. It allows you to face your demons, make them tangible, and expel them. It allows you to understand why you do what you do and think how you think. Writing has been known to be therapeutic for the mind and soul and have significant effects on the body. Study after study shows how depression and grief can be combated and even overcome by people sharing and processing their stories. In short, writing has the power to change your life, as well as the lives of others, if only you could learn how to use it. There are several concepts to keep in mind as you begin this journey:

1. You do not have to be a good writer or know proper grammar to be an effective writer for your writing to be impactful; however, you can prevent miscommunication if you know how to write.
2. You do not need to publicize or share your writing for it to serve a purpose.
3. In your writing, you do not need to be politically correct or give canned or expected responses; rather, it is more effective when you speak your heart and be honest with yourself.
4. Journaling is not a form of writing where you do not have to fake it or portray an image. It's about being real.

Guidelines for this Writing Program

1. The goal of this writing study is self discovery and reflection. It is not designed to tell you how to solve all of life's problems or reveal some grand advice from renowned experts. Rather, no one is an expert on your own life except you. You are the master. As William Ernest Henley writes in "Invictus": "I am the master of my fate: I am the captain of my soul." Make this your mantra as you move through this study, as it is designed to be a journey in which you are indeed the captain—of both your fate and your soul. There is no greater truth in your life than this. No one can guide your life's ship any better than you can. Hopefully, this study can chart new waters for you.
2. This study is not a race. It is designed for one lesson per week, but you can set your own pace. However, the more time you reflect on each lesson, the more meaningful it will be. The hope is that you read the lesson and then spend the week writing and reflecting on it. The questions are designed to serve as springboards for your reflections, but you are encouraged to write beyond the scope of what they address.

3. Attempt every question; however, if a question causes pain or emotion that you are not prepared to face, skip it. You can always come back to it later (or not at all).

4. Be as honest with yourself as you can in your responses.

5. Keep in mind that even if you take every step to ensure your writing will be private, there may come a time when someone, even without your permission, will read it. Do not write anything that might lead to consequences you are not prepared to face. If you write about your intentions to harm someone or yourself and someone reads that, there will be an intervention. While you are encouraged to be transparent, you need to be careful with how much you share, given that your personal property may be searched and your reflections read in your current environment.

6. Do not worry about writing conventions in your responses. This is not a grammar or composition class.

7. Keep in mind that writing is dependent on your current state of mind. Feelings and emotions are variable and change from day to day, sometimes even hour to hour, depending on your circumstances. What you write one day may not reflect how you feel the next.

8. The key to journaling is grace and space. Give yourself both.

9. Writing is one aspect of your life that cannot be controlled or imprisoned by anyone. As long as you have a pen and paper, you can write anywhere, any time, any place. You have complete control over what you write; however, remember there are always consequences to every action, even writing.

10. Do not put pressure on yourself to write or complete a lesson. If you aren't feeling it on a certain day, then don't force it. Take a break and come back to it when you are in a better place mentally and emotionally.

Writing for Reflection

- *Why do you want to engage in this writing study?*

- *Do you journal?*

- *Do you write creatively on your own (i.e. a novel, short stories, poetry)?*

- *Do you have other opportunities to write regularly? (i.e. educational programs, classes, workshops, job-related documents). Explain.*

- *Do you have any prior experience with writing? If so, describe.*

- *Do you enjoy reflection and introspection? Explain.*

- *What are your feelings about writing?*

- *Do you have any writing goals?*

- *How much time do you think you can devote to writing per week?*

Our Stories

My Story. Although my story is not as important as yours, it bears knowing so you will understand why this course was created. First, I have some experience being on the inside, or as some call it, behind the walls. No, I have never committed a crime worthy of imprisonment and have never served one day before bars as an offender. Have I made some major mistakes in my life? Yep. Am I screw-up? Yes. Am I broken? Yes, contrary to what some may think about themselves, we all are—some obviously more than others. The thing about prison is that if you are incarcerated, you cannot deny the fact that you are broken, whereas those of us on the outside often do everything in our power to make ourselves appear unbroken.

This is one thing I find refreshing about inmates: they are not afraid to face their brokenness. Through a prison education program, I was able to work with convicted robbers, drug dealers, murderers, sex offenders, and rapists on a regular basis. I heard their stories and saw firsthand what they faced. I tried in all the ways I knew how to better their lives, even if they were never going to see life on the streets again. I witnessed a prison riot through the windows of a classroom office, watching corrections officers sprinting to the mayhem in an effort to prevent people from getting hurt. I saw the sun's rays hitting rows of white crosses looming over graves where inmates after death were lost and discarded by family members. I saw broken arms and cancer go untreated for months. I saw inmates' prized possessions being ransacked and destroyed for no reason. Prison is indeed one of the most horrible and terrifying places on this earth, and those who say otherwise are flat out ignorant.

To say that this experience changed me is an understatement. Spending time in prison taught me several realities about the people in there. The most important: these people, including you, are human beings with emotions, feelings, thoughts, goals, hopes, and dreams, even if these were broken in some way. I do not discount that there are many serving time who deserve to remain there for the rest of their lives. They have become hardened and bitter, and they choose not to change. However, there are others who can and do want to be better and are trying everything they can to make that happen. Their stories are the ones that need to be changed. Their stories are the ones that matter. Your story. This rest of this lesson is devoted to your story—not just your crime, but your story. The questions that follow will provide an outline for your story.

Your Before

- Describe your childhood.
- Describe your life before you became incarcerated.
- Write a profile of that person in the third person (i.e. John was a mild-mannered child…")
- What are some qualities you would change about that person?
- What factors led you down a path that led to incarceration?
- Was there anything you could have done to change that path?
- Were there key people who contributed to the decisions that led you down this path?
- Were there people who were trying to help you that you disregarded?

The Crime

- What crime did you commit to land you in prison?
- What circumstances led you to commit your crime?
- What were your feelings at the time of the incident?
- What could you have changed to prevent yourself from committing your crime?
- Will you someday be released from prison?
- If you have been released from prison, where are you living? What are your current circumstances?

Your Day-to-Day Life in Prison

- What are the biggest obstacles to peace you face in your current situation?
- Is there anything you can do to change this?
- What are the biggest dangers you face in your current situation?
- Is there anything you can do to change this?
- Do you have anything you look forward to when you get up each morning? If so, what? How often are you allowed to enjoy these?

- Do you have daily goals? If not, why? If so, do you write these down?
- What do you do on a typical day in your current life?
- What are the sources of current stress in your life?

Your Feelings

- Record your feelings both at the time of the incident that landed you in prison and now as you reflect on it.
- Are these feelings the same or different? How have they changed?
- Describe your current mental state. Is there anything you can do to change it?
- Would you classify yourself as a hopeful person, even given your current circumstances?
- Would you say you are a person who is in touch with your feelings? Explain.
- List the feelings you might feel on any given day in your current life.
- What are some people, places, activities, or things that might bring you joy, peace, or other positive feelings? Is there anything you can do to bring these things into your life?

Your Goals

- What are your goals today?
- What are your short-term goals, as in this month?
- What are your goals for the year?
- Where do you see yourself in five years?
- What are some steps you can take to achieve those goals?
- If you have no goals, why?
- If you have no goals, what are some goals that you could possibly strive for, even some you may not have considered?

Your Tribe

- Do you have a support system inside? Explain.
- Are these individuals a good influence or not? Explain.
- Do these individuals support you? Explain.
- Do these individuals make you happy? Explain.
- Do these individuals make a positive impact on your physical well-being? Explain.

- Do these individuals make a positive impact on your mental well-being? Explain.
- Do you have a support system outside? Explain.
- Are these individuals a good influence or not? Explain.
- Do these individuals support you? Explain.
- Do these individuals make you happy? Explain.
- Do these individuals make a positive impact on your physical well-being? Explain.
- Do these individuals make a positive impact on your mental well-being? Explain.

Your Future
- Do you see a future for yourself? Explain.
- Describe that future in terms of people in your life. Whom do you see in your future?
- Describe that future in terms of peace. Are you content? If not, why?
- Describe that future in terms of a job. Do you see yourself having a job or vocation? If so, what is it?
- Describe your ideal future with no limits.
- Describe your ideal future within the reality of your current state.
- What are some steps within your control that you can take to make your ideal future a reality?

The Human Story—The Problem

You may or may not be a person of faith; regardless of what you believe, you cannot deny the fact that we as a human race are a pretty messed up bunch of creatures. Fundamental questions from humans—even those who lived long ago— have often centered around where we came from and what happens to the intangible part of us after we die. What is the reason we are here? What is our purpose? And why are we prone to sinful behavior, often repeating mistakes that will in the end, cause us and others pain? At the end of the day, there are several realities from which we cannot hide about the human condition.

Every human sins and commits wrongdoings. While no one will ever downplay or excuse the crimes you have committed—nor should they—you are not alone in that you are a sinful person; every single human alive is guilty of sin. Granted, many of the sins committed by the average person do not land them in prison. Lies, gossip, theft, jealousy, angry outbursts, emotional pain inflicted on people we love…the list of actions and emotions brought about by our sinful nature is long and varied. Some of these actions and emotions have the ability to hurt people and even at times destroy lives.

Granted, most people have not had to serve time in prison to account for these kinds of sins. But you have. Every single day, you pay for your crimes. Your daily life is payment for the wrongdoings you committed. You get up, put one foot in front of the other, and face what you did. Every day is a price paid to your debt to society. Granted, you have no control over payment of that debt. You were forced, rightfully so, into this. Unless you have been falsely imprisoned, you hurt people in some way, likely innocent people, and you will have to live with that for the rest of your life. No one can spare you from that. However, your response to how you deal with that payment is up to you—and you alone. As the popular life tenant goes, "Do not judge someone until you have walked a mile in their shoes." Quite frankly, I have not walked in your shoes. I have never been emotionally or physically abused by someone I love. I have never had to steal to eat. I have never been neglected by people who should have taken care of me and provided for my basic needs. I did not grow up in a home where my parents were drug addicts or murderers. God, the universe, or whatever you believe about our creation, spared me from that. But if I had been born in—and walked in your shoes—I cannot say with absolute certainty that I would not have made decisions similar to what you did. I would like to say that I would have been smarter, more compassionate, or less violent than you in that situation, but I cannot say for certain. Like you, I am the sum of my life experiences and the environment in which I was raised, and I was blessed beyond measure. Many of us are. But without those amazing influences—a loving family, a solid education, fulfillment of my basic physical and emotional needs—what would I have become? No one can say for certain. But I will say this: if you want to wallow in your past, your future will look just as dismal, and you have no one to blame but yourself for every decision you make as you move forward.

Hurt (adjective) people hurt (verb) people. This is a premise that can probably account for the majority of every kind of problem in our world. When a person has been hurt by someone, even in one of the most basic ways, the tendency is to lash out at someone else. Think about a time when you stubbed your toe or cut your finger. You likely didn't look to the person next to you and tell them how much fun you were having or how great they made you feel. You probably said a few swear words, yelled, and even threw something across the room or banged your hand down on a counter.

Pain begets pain, and that is a life truth. Chances are probably good that you committed your crime because you were hurting, either in an overt way that you could identify, or in a way that you may not have even known. Deeply rooted pain often goes untreated and manifests itself in violent ways. It is widely known that sexual offenders were most likely sexually abused or molested themselves. Abusers were often abused themselves as children, often by caregivers or other people close to them. If you have gone through a course offered by prison officials that allowed you to face and deal with your crime, you likely learned all about this.

There is, in all of us, inherent good and evil. Although "good" and "evil" are abstract terms and hard to define, every one of us has the ability to be good humans, bad humans, or downright evil humans. Sometimes we can be all three on the same day. We receive this classification based on the way we treat people, our choices and their subsequent consequences, and the perceptions of others based on how we live our lives.

While some people think they are destined to be only one or the other, all of us have times in our lives when we have done something—even something considered minor, such as gossip about our friend—that puts us in the "bad" category. Or we give money to a homeless person, which puts us in the "good" category. You probably think, due to the crimes you have committed, that you are a bad or even evil person; even if you do not, chances are that someone else thinks that about you. While the crimes you committed are indeed bad and likely caused pain to others in some way, they do not define you. Your actions and choices can be categorized as good or bad, but you do not have to fit that role. You are not locked into the path you have charted for yourself and can change direction at any time. Even if you or others think of you as being "bad", you are completely capable of doing good things and making good choices. Conversely, what most would consider "good" people can make bad decisions. There are even times when the world can see a person one way, but the reality is entirely the opposite. We have seen this in politics and throughout history over and over again.

We may have moments in life where we find ourselves questioning why bad things happen to good people or good things happen to bad people. This is an ages-long, universal life question that has plagued just about every sane human at some point in their lives. The fact is: there is no answer to this question; there is no why. The reality is that *things* happen to *people*. It is as simple and as complicated as that. We need to realize that things—good and bad—are going to happen to people—good and bad— and sometimes there is little that can be done to stop these from taking place. However, again, we can control what we do with those "things", and how we use them to set the tone for our future thoughts and actions.

You have free will to decide whether your actions will be good or bad. If you choose to give into the criminal mentality, that is your choice, but you have the option to choose the opposite. My experiences in the prison have shown me that oftentimes, you may have to make what most consider "bad" choices just to stay safe—and sometimes even alive. Even if you have to do that to stay alive, remember, at your core, you don't have to be that person. You can choose to be a good person at any stage in your life, no matter how old you are or what you have done. The past is over and done with you, and you cannot change that. However, you can change the now—and who you are today.

You have to remember that every single choice has a consequence—both good and bad. Even what you may think of as the most trivial choices in your daily life will have a consequence. For example, the route I choose to take home from work will have a consequence. One route may be a safe one; however, I may encounter an intoxicated driver on another. If I choose to take one road, I will end up home safely. If I take the other, I could encounter the intoxicated driver and end up in the hospital—or even the morgue. The restaurant where I choose to eat dinner might result in a regular night at home watching TV afterward or a night in the ER from food poisoning. It is scary to think about, but even the most minutest of decisions can have the most serious and life-changing consequences.

The same holds true for more important decisions, such as whether you want to make what most would consider good changes in your life—or keep repeating mistakes out of habit or because you fear change. You already know what happens when you choose poorly. You have seen this play out firsthand in your own life in the most extreme way. You pay for your poor choices every single day you wake up. Some of your cellmates or others you know may have even paid for those choices with their lives. If you are not prepared for the consequence of a bad choice, then the decision is simple: don't make it. It's not rocket science, but if every single person on the planet remembered this, the world would have fewer problems—and our prisons would be less crowded.

At the end of the day, every decision you make—good and bad—all comes back to one thing: your why. Why do you exist? Why do you get up every day? Why do you eat what you eat? Why do you spend time with the people you do? Why do you work a job or take part in a hobby? Why make the decisions you do? Why do you experience the feelings you do? Every decision you make, consciously or subconsciously, has a why behind it.

Writing for Reflection

- *Do you currently feel broken? Explain.*

- *Do you see past hurts as one of the reasons you committed the crime(s) that you did?*

- *Do you see past hurts contributing to your present decisions?*

- *What or whom caused your pain?*

- *At your core, do you classify yourself as a good or a bad person?*

- *At your core, who do you want to be?*

- *When you find yourself making bad choices, what is the motivation behind these choices?*

- *What, if anything, can you do to prevent yourself from making bad decisions?*

- *What steps can you take to ensure that you make good decisions?*

- *What steps can you take to change your current path and focus on the present?*

Your *Why*

At the end of the day, you must determine your why—the overarching why that Infiltrates every aspect of your daily life. Your why will drive every present and future decision you make and what you make of the days—and hopefully years—you have left on this planet. The hard part is that no one can help you figure out your why but you. You alone can chart your path.

Sadly, most people do not take the time or put in the effort to figure out their why. They live the majority of their lives based on tradition, expectation, habit, uncertainty, or the inability to figure anything else out. They live in the cities where they grew up because that is where they were born. They go to college because that is what their parents or society expects of them. They work at jobs they detest because they need a paycheck and think they have no other options to pay the bills. They celebrate traditions and holidays because the rest of the world does. They take part in their daily routine because that is what they have always done. They commit crimes because their parents or friends did, and a life of criminality is all they know. Maybe this is you.

While living a life solely built on routine and habit—devoid of introspection or reflection—is not particularly bad in all cases, living life in this way does not foster innovation or passion. It does not invigorate you or motivate you to live your life to the fullest, to help you develop your talents, to allow you to experience joy and peace over the simplest of life's experiences, or to discover the best version of yourself.

So why don't more people delve into their why? Because the overwhelming "why" question is one of the hardest ones to address—let alone answer. However, if you take the time to explore your why, you might be surprised by what you discover about yourself—and the motivation that drives your decisions and actions. It might even explain how you ended up where you did—and how you can avoid repeating those mistakes in the future.

Humans crave purpose. Among the many of life's most perplexing and unanswered questions is the reason for human existence. No one to date has discovered an answer to this question, although followers of the main world religions have all weighed in an answer. In reality, none of us will find out the answer to this question until it is answered upon our death. Even those with the most devout belief systems cannot say that they absolutely know what will happen when they pass from this earth. Yes, they can conjecture and cleave strongly to their certainty of an afterlife; some may even have had near-death experiences where their physical body died briefly and then was resuscitated. However, we do not know with absolute certainty what will happen to us when our brains stop working or even why we are here in the first place—what exactly is our purpose?

However, reflecting on the sources that drive us individually can at least lend purpose to our own lives; I think just about every human alive would like to define the answer to their own question of purpose. Even if we are not aware of it consciously, we crave purpose and meaning. Most of us want to know that, during the numbered days we have on this planet, we have contributed something to this world—that someone cared that we were here.

This is one of the reasons people crave fame and fortune. Making a contribution to entertainment, government, music, art, or writing immortalizes us. Think about some of the most famous people you know of: Elvis Presley, Leonardo da Vinci, George Washington, Edgar Allen Poe, William Shakespeare—and as much as some haters want to deny, even Taylor Swift. Even though you have never met any of these people, and some of them only lived for a few decades, their contributions to our society have allowed them to live on in ways most of us never will. Their sense of purpose led them to do and create things that will allow them to live for centuries, even though most of their earthly bodies, Swift excluded, have long perished. This comes back to your purpose—your why.

Another characteristic of humanity is that humans are made to create. If you are a believer in God, you believe that humans are created in his likeness. And if He is the ultimate creator, then you, as a human, have an innate desire to create, even if you do not feel like you possess the gift of creativity. You create something every day, even if you do not realize it. Even in your current environment, restricted as it is, you create daily routines, contemplate reasons for your actions, and seek ways of completing tasks in your cell and at your job, if you have one. These all involve the process of creation. Some of you create meals out of chow food and items purchased in the canteen. Some of you create workout routines to remain fit and healthy, even though resources are limited. Some of you create song lists on devices that you are able to possess. Some of you attend high school and college classes and create projects for assignments. Some of you may even take part in various artistic endeavors: you write, you draw, you paint, you make music, you sing, and you play an instrument, if given the opportunity.

Even though you do not have control over your environment, you have control over your response to this environment. This reality, although more common sense than advanced or deep thinking, is one people often forget when faced with adversity. Like we all do at times, you may be one to blame your circumstances for why you behave in the way you do. Something or someone else is at fault—childhood, abuse, addiction, parents, the corrupt law system, discrimination, lack of education, inept professionals, the wrong wrong crowd, lack of income, and other factors—when you make a bad choice or find yourself in a precarious situation. The reality is that often you cannot control many external factors in life, such as where you were born or live, who your parents are, what color your skin is, and how much education you received. You most certainly cannot control the prison environment in which you currently reside.

However, you can control how you react to this environment. Yes, it is easy for me to say that I would make good decisions in your place because the reality is that I am not in your place. It is easy for us on the outside to tell you to avoid the gangs, the drugs, and the other negative influences you face daily and choose the straight-and-narrow path. I know enough about prison life to know that many choose this path because it is easier; others choose this path because it means they get to stay alive.

Humans are creatures of habit. Another aspect of the human condition that makes life challenging at times is that we crave consistency; hence, most of what we do every day we do out of habit. Bad habits are hard to break, and conversely good, healthy habits are difficult to start, especially if they feel foreign to us. This is one of the biggest reasons why people have a hard time breaking a bad habit like overeating or smoking cigarettes, and why they have a hard time building up a good habit such as an exercise routine. Most of us have created and built life-long habits that control our lives, and those habits are hard to change. If we are lucky and they are good, then they will likely lead to healthier, more productive aspects of our lives. If they are destructive habits, then we often have to suffer painful consequences of those.

Fear is one of the most powerful of human forces. When fear takes over, it can cause normal, stable people to make rash, destructive decisions or act in a way that is contrary to how they might ordinarily behave. It may be possible that fear was the force that drove you to commit your crime. Often the response to fear is instinctual, and we have little control over how we respond in situations where we feel afraid. The fight or flight response that is engrained in all of us is what causes us to jump or swing our arms in the air when we are startled unexpectedly, even if there is no real or present danger. It may cause us to lash out physically if we feel threatened by another individual or a wild animal. While many of us may not be able to control how we react in a moment where our lives are visibly threatened, we should be aware of how powerful fear can be. It is always good to have a plan or response in place if we find ourselves in a situation where we might be physically or emotionally harmed—or worse.

So, as we reflect on these ideas, take some time to think about your why. Think about your purpose, your creative endeavors, your habits, and your fears. Reflect on how they have shaped you and which of these you have the power to change.

Writing for Reflection

- *Do have a faith in a creator or believe in organized religion? Explain.*

- *Have you ever given thought as to why you are here on this earth?*

- *Do you feel like humans were created for a purpose? If so, can you elaborate on what that purpose is?*

- *Do you feel like **you** were created for a purpose?*

- *What forces drive your daily decisions?*

- *If you had to explain why you arose out of your bed today, what would you say?*

- *Do you have any contribution that you make to this world that would make it a better place?*

- *Would you define yourself as a creative person? Why/why not?*

- *What kinds of things do you create daily?*

- *How do you typically respond when faced with adversity or challenges? Would you like to change this behavior? Why/why not?*

- *How do you respond when someone hurts you, either physically or emotionally? Would you like to change this behavior? Why/why not?*

- *List your bad habits. List your good habits.*

- *List any bad habits that you would like to expunge from your life? Do you have any plan to do this?*

- *List any good habits that you currently do not have but would like to? What can you do to practice those habits?*

Changing Your Narrative: Know Your Worth

There are many theories that span years as to why people behave in the ways they do and why they become the kind of person they become. Some theorists claim we were born with traits that cause us to behave in certain ways; others say the environmental factors in which we were born and raised play the biggest role. Still others claim that who and what we become are a combination of these and other factors, such as unexpected life events that may transform us at any stage in our lives.

Regardless of these factors, there is one tenet that most—but not all—cultures hold to be true: every human life has worth. Hence why some of the most volatile of political and social debates rage over issues related to the value of human life. Such questions cannot easily be answered. These questions range from beginning-of-life issues to end-of-life issues and everything in between. These are indeed the hard ones and include: When does human life actually begin? What right does a woman have to destroy a life growing within her own body? Who should live—the mother or the baby—if life hangs in the balance for both? Do people have the right to humanely end their own life if they are suffering from a terminal illness? Should someone who has taken a life have their own life taken? Should a baby in the womb that shows physical deformities or mental deficiencies be allowed to live? Should those who show no brain activity due to an accident be supported through artificial, life-saving means? Do people who are unable to walk or speak have a quality of life? Should parents bring other children into this world for the sole purpose of saving another one's life? Should human organs be harvested to save the lives of others? Should humans be cloned?

When it comes to human life, the list of questions related to ethics is never ending. However, most people would agree that as long as a person is breathing, they deserve a shot at living and also that their life has value. I know that some of you have harmed or maybe even taken a human life. I am not here to shame you for that. That is between you and yourself or you and your creator. And, as I have mentioned before, you are paying for that action. Despite this, however, you still have a purpose. Your life still has value. You cannot change the past (another topic we will discuss in a later lesson), but you can change the present, and thus the future. You need to realize that despite your gravest and most horrific mistakes, your life has value—you have value. Just as importantly, the good decisions you make moving forward can impact the world for good. If you are truly sorry and repentant for what you did in the past, then change. You may have heard this before, but the most heartfelt of apologies manifest themselves in true change. While you will never be able to make up for the harm you caused others in your past, you can offset that with good decisions as you move forward with the rest of your life. If you do, there are hopefully some realizations you may come to.

You have the ability to be a kind person. I am not here to preach religion, but I have a firm belief that just as pain begets pain, love begets love. While you may not believe in a higher power or believe that someone cares about you, I have seen lives transformed because of love. I am not talking about a romantic, fairy-tale kind of love. I am talking about the kind of love that humans have for each other, deep down, that bubbles to the surface when times are rough. This is the kind of love that causes total strangers to risk their lives pulling someone out of a burning car on the side of the highway after an accident. This is the kind of love that causes people on a social media platform to donate millions of dollars to a child with cancer whom they have never met. This is the kind of love that causes service men and women to risk their lives for our freedom, knowing they will receive little in return. This love is a part of the human DNA, and it is part of your DNA too, even if you don't want to admit or acknowledge it. It may be buried under years of abuse or pain, but it still is there. This is why you have worth. You have the capability to love and be loved, even if you don't feel like it.

You will be surprised what happens in your life if you think you have worth. Even if you have screwed up your life miserably, you do not have to be an a**hole moving forward. You have the power and control to change your attitude and behavior toward other people. I know change is hard. I know prison is a dark place, where sometimes there exists a "kill-or-be-killed" way of life. I know you might be living in the type of prison where drugs and gang wars are rampant, and bad things happen to nice people.

However, continuing to repeat bad behaviors and purposely lashing out at everyone in your world can only snowball and keep you on the hamster wheel of a bad decision/ bad consequence cycle.

I can say from my personal experience in the prison environment that I have respect for the offenders I have worked with who respect both me and themselves. I attempt to be their biggest cheerleader, even on days where they slip up and do not make the best decisions. I have seen their overall will to change and better their lives, and I believe that I and others like me have hope for those who demonstrate hope for themselves. Hope is contagious, and so is a good attitude.

I know it is easy for me to sit here from the comfort of my free world and tell you that believing in yourself and hence making better decisions involve a simple change of attitude that you can turn on like a light switch. I don't believe this—even for people who don't live in your toxic world. Changing your mindset and improving your self-confidence takes years of hard work—often work that is simply too hard to put in. However, you have to start somewhere. Big change comes with little steps.

As we established in a previous lesson, even if you don't have control over your environment, you have control over your emotions and responses to that environment. If you are a person who likes concrete examples, look at it like this. Let's say that your psyche is composed of a house with different rooms. Each of these rooms represents different emotions (such as peace, anger, anxiety, joy, guilt, etc.) Although our society has made huge strides in technology, we have not yet discovered the ability to be present in several places at the same time. As a result, at any given moment in time, you have to choose the mental room where you will reside. Applying this concept to my illustration means that you have to choose your emotion at any given time. You may not have a lot of control over what is happening to you right now, but you can choose the room where you will spend your time. If you currently find yourself hanging out in a negative room, such as guilt or anger, get out of that room. Turn off the light, close the door, and choose a different room. Go to a room where you feel like the best version of yourself. Choose a room of peace. Choose a room of kindness. Choose a room of patience. Choose a better room.

Writing for Reflection

- *Discuss your level of self-worth.*

- *What factors have contributed to your self-worth?*

- *Do you believe that you were born with traits that resulted in your bad decisions?*

- *Do you believe that environmental factors (such as family, poverty, abuse, etc.) led to your bad decisions?*

- *How do you currently treat other offenders?*

- *How do you currently treat others with whom you come in contact (officers, unit team leaders, cooks, medical personnel, education staff)?*

- *Do you feel respected by other offenders? Why/why not?*

- *Do you feel respected by staff? Why/why not?*

- *Are there behaviors you can change that might encourage those around you to respect and value you more?*

- *In what "room" or "rooms" do you most frequently reside?*

- *What steps can you take to move to a room where you will be happier and healthier?*

Changing Your Narrative: Embrace the Present

We are often reminded that the only day that matters is today—that we cannot change the past nor are we guaranteed the future. Hence, living in the past—either reliving the good days or lamenting the bad ones—is not a healthy practice. Likewise, stressing about the future is not very conducive to our mental health, either. For one, the future isn't here yet, and when it is, it will be the present. And second, we can only do so much to control the outcome of our future.

So how do we embrace the present? Such is not the easiest task. Life moves at a brisk pace these days, especially the older we get; it is hard to stay grounded in the present moment. You may have heard of a popular buzzword that permeates the self-help realm these days: mindfulness. While entire books have been written about this, the concept boils down to one simple life tip: be present in the present. People who lived a decade or two ago were probably better at this than our current age and likely practiced this every day without realizing it. They didn't have the modern-day distractions that we have and were more adept at focusing on the simple joys of life that we have replaced with dopamine rushes brought about by binge watching and mindless scrolling.

Practice mindfulness. So what does it mean to practice mindfulness? More importantly, what does it mean for you as an inmate behind bars? Essentially, it means the same for you as it does for me or anyone living in this world. Live in the present. Don't focus on the past or the future. Pay attention to what is going on around you in ways you might not ordinarily. Ground in the now. When you are drinking a cup of coffee, pay attention to its taste and texture. When you are waking up to start your day, pay attention to what you are feeling and thinking. Listen to the sounds around you. Listen to your body. Stop letting your mind wander or allowing yourself to get caught up in the drama around you.

There are many forms of mindfulness. Some strategies involve sitting still and listening to the body, focusing on one part of your body at a time and immersing yourself in the feelings that come with that focus. Others involve breath work, where you pay close attention to your breathing and breathe in certain ways so you can connect to your body better. Still others involve exercises where you take in your surroundings, writing down what you see on a daily basis, and taking note of the details that you might ordinarily overlook. Most of all, it involves removing distractions that prevent you from connecting to others so that whatever is in front of you has your full attention.

How can mindfulness help you? First off, it has been shown to do wonders for the body. If done consistently, it can improve blood pressure and help with anxiety. It can make you more relaxed and focused. While multitasking is often praised in this current social climate, it is not always the healthiest thing for us as it can lead to increased levels of stress. Focusing on one thing at a time often removes us from that flight or flight feeling that comes with increased levels of the stress hormone, cortisol, in our bodies. Too much of this in our body leads to weight gain, increased blood pressure, heart issues, and many other health ailments.

Secondly, if you are busy focusing on the present and taking in everything around you, you don't have time or energy to expend on negativity. Mindfulness draws you away from other negative influences that can wear you down and lead you to make poor decisions that are not in your best interest. If you are focusing on relaxation, you also don't have time to be a jerk to people.

Finally, mindfulness can allow you to reside in the emotional "rooms" where your heart and mind can remain at peace. This is all important if you are going to remain grounded in your current environment. If you want to make better choices and get to know the better version of you, you need to immerse yourself in positive emotions rather than negative ones.

Practice gratitude. I know you may find the concept of gratitude rather ironic given your current plight in life. Despite this, I know this may sound harsh, but you have breath, and your heart is currently beating. You got up today, and although it may not have been a good day, you still had a roof over your head and food to eat. You likely have people on the outside who care about you. You have the beautiful, amazing gift of health. I can tell you that in this day and age, health is a real gift. There is not a day that goes by when I don't hear about or read about a family, friend, or acquaintance contracting yet another form of cancer. These are people of all ages and all walks of life too. You have the mental ability to learn and grow, to form better habits, and make better decisions. You have the gift of this moment and hopefully a string of hundreds of moments all woven together to create a better future.

Many of you may be released from prison in the future (or you already are), and you will have a second shot—a second chance—at a whole new life. Yes, you will have scars and blemishes, but we all do. You can use those to make you better and stronger. You can also use your time while in prison wisely before you are given your freedom. Create habits now that will be carried over when you find yourself with more control over your life. Practice at being the best version of you so you can discover the best version of you.

Others of you who must remain in prison for life can choose to become mentors and role models for those who come after you. You can impact the people around you and show them that you can be a positive influence in a not-so-positive environment. A friend of mine recently shared her husband's motto that was great life advice: "As long as you are on this side of the dirt, you can do anything you want to do." This can be you. After all, what do you have to lose by becoming a better person? If God exists and there is an afterlife—a heaven and hell—then you will have a better shot at going to the better of the two. If there is no god, then at least you have made your life less complicated here; along the way, you might even make life better for a few other people, which is a whole lot better than being an a**hole.

Forgive yourself. Replace guilt with acceptance. Forgiveness is a common, multifaceted issue in the corrections environment. When convicted killers on death row are presented in movies facing execution, the family members of those who were killed are often shown, sitting there waiting for what they might deem as justice. Viewers often wonder: did the family forgive the offender, or were they vindicated only when they were allowed to see the accused breathe their last? Most of all, did the convicted killers show remorse and/or were they able to forgive themselves? There is a sad, morbid fascination with the concept of forgiveness, especially when the issue of the death penalty arises.

If you are remorseful for the crimes you have committed, it might be hard to move on without the forgiveness of those you wronged (or their family members if the victims are deceased). The first step is to strive for and seek this kind of forgiveness from those you have wronged; however, just like you cannot control your environment, you cannot control other people. Those you wronged may never come to a place of forgiveness, and if they don't, you need to move on from that. The inability to forgive someone almost always creates another kind of prison—more emotional than physical— and that is not your problem.

You can only do so much to earn forgiveness, and at some point, the decision is out of your hands. Even if others you wronged are not able to forgive you, as hard as it is, you can still forgive yourself. At the end of the day, there is only one person you have to look in the mirror—one person you have to go to bed with each night and wake up to each morning. You need to come to a place where you must be able to forgive yourself. If you are truly remorseful, at some point you have to let it go. It is far easier said than done. However, remember, all of us in life have made some painful and regretful mistakes. We all have decisions we wish we could take back or moments we could redo. If life had a rewind button, oh how much better it would be. The key here, however, is this: if you could have the ability to rewind some of your actions, would you have made a different decision, even if you had the assurance you would not get caught? Or would you have moved ahead anyway, prepared to face the consequences you now have experienced?

Thoughts are not facts or reality. As hard as it is to understand, our thoughts and feelings are not facts or reality. This is often hard to remember because for many of us, our thoughts are the only reality we know. However, we have to remember that just because we think a certain way or feel a certain emotion, this does not mean that everyone else feels the same. This is one of the biggest issues our country is facing today. So many people think that if someone disagrees with them or does not experience the same emotion they do in a given situation, then those people are ignorant or out of touch. If they don't share their beliefs, then they are wrong. Life—and all of its components—is not always black or white; rather, it's full of gray. We are in many ways gray beings, each of us different with different belief systems, different ways of expressing emotions, and different experiences. Be kind to your fellow gray beings.

Writing for Reflection

- *Do you have a hard time focusing on the present? Why/why not?*

- *Do you often find yourself reliving the past? If so, what events are foremost in your mind?*

- *Do you find yourself worrying about the future? If so, what concerns you most about the future?*

- *What do you know about mindfulness? Have you ever practiced it?*

- *What are some ways you can practice mindfulness, even given your limitations?*

- *What are some steps you can take to be more present in the moment?*

- *Are you a grateful person? If not, why? If so, what factors led you to become so?*

- *What are some people, places, or things for which you are grateful?*

- *What are some ways you can practice a lifestyle of gratitude?*

- *Have you sought forgiveness from those you have wronged? If so, were you forgiven for the sins/crimes you have committed by those you wronged?*

- *Have you forgiven yourself for your past? Explain.*

- *What are some ways you can work to move on and forgive yourself, if you have not already?*

Changing Your Narrative: Learn to Learn

One of the first action steps you can take to change your narrative is to take advantage of the resources that are available to you. While I don't pretend to know the prison culture, I know there are resources on the inside that can help you make better decisions. From religious organizations to educational opportunities, you can take part in activities that will help you avoid the dark side of prison life. Often these will get you out of the cell houses for long periods of time and put you in contact with people on the outside who are invested in you and care about you.

It may seem cliche, but reading can open up a whole new world for you. Read everything you can get your hands on. This cannot be stressed enough. If you are not cut out or do not have the time for a rigorous educational program, there is nothing to stop you from reading. Reading can also improve your mind and open up new areas of learning for you. Most prisons have on-site libraries from which you can check out books. Ask family members of friends on the outside to purchase books that you might find interesting. Look for books that stimulate your mind and curiosity. Look for books that can help you learn the answers to questions you may have in life. Read as much and as often as you can. Set reading goals for yourself; strive to reach a reading goal. For example, try to read so many pages a day or a certain number of books a month. Keep a record or log of your reading. Most importantly, do not underestimate the power of reading—and all the benefits that can result from it.

Get an education. Education can be life-changing, which I have seen firsthand. If you have the ability to get an education, by all means, take advantage of it. Education will empower and equip you. If you do not have your high school diploma, get it, or enroll in a GED program. If you already have this, then pursue a college degree, if a program is available in your prison. Many colleges and universities offer degrees in prison programs as part of the Pell Grant program. The benefits to this decision are countless.

Educational opportunities lower recidivism rates. Studies have unanimously demonstrated that educational programs in prisons lower recidivism rates. This means that when you are educated, you have a lesser chance of returning to prison or reoffending once you are freed.

Education will teach you life skills that can be valuable to you in a professional setting and in other areas of your life. In addition to the content you will learn from the various subjects you study, there are other skills you will learn in a classroom setting that are difficult to learn elsewhere in life, especially in a prison environment. Education leads to improved literacy, along with discipline, critical thinking, creative thinking, reading, problem-solving, study skills, and memorization strategies. One important statistic that cannot be overlooked is the large number of incarcerated individuals who struggle with literacy and critical thinking skills.

Being in classes provides hope and motivation. Peer mentoring in the educational setting provides good role models; skills learned also are also shown to help you cope with prison, and many of you will experience improved family relationships. When you are given the opportunity to attend class and, as a result grow mentally, it helps you emotionally as well.

Classes within prison give you something productive to do and occupy your mind. One of the reasons violence is so prevalent in prisons is because many inmates literally have nothing to do. While some inmates do work in prison jobs during the day, many do not, leaving them with large blocks of unproductive time.

According to research, one of the top three reasons that inmates enroll in coursework is to occupy their time, noting that many prisoners enroll in an Adult Continuing Education class every day to have something to do. If nothing else, taking classes will get you out of your cell house. The more opportunities you have to get away from the cell houses and away from people who might not be particularly good influences on your life, the better off you will be.

Education provides opportunities that you may have been deprived of when you were younger. Unfortunately, there is a direct correlation between education and incarceration. Many of you who committed violent crimes did so because you grew up in poverty and had no hopes of gaining an education, and as a result, gainful employment to better your life. Getting an education now can change this trajectory.

Coursework provides job skills that will help you post-release. Research indicates that literacy and numeracy skills improve among prisoners who take part in academic programs. This can translate into critical thinking and other job skills that will help you once you get out of prison and transition into the workforce. Again, if a program can offer an alternative to a crime-ridden life and provide a means for you to obtain good employment after release, you will be less likely to return to a life of crime, and as a result, less likely to return to prison. The job market is competitive as it is, and it is not a surprise that having a prison record is not going to work in your favor. Having a degree—and the skills and discipline that accompany it—can help you find a job that will better support you and a family. It will also allow you to show something for your time behind bars.

Educated inmates can make positive differences within their communities—both in and out of prison. It is my hope—and the hope of others like me who educate prisoners—that those I teach will somehow pay it forward if they find themselves eventually freed from prison. I want all of them to make a positive difference to those they encounter both while still in prison and post-release. Education—and along with it the myriad of skills it embodies—will give you the tools to do that. It gives you an equal playing field with those who were educated as children and young adults.

Education humanizes those confined within prison walls and provides purpose and value. At the end of the day, as the first part of this study discussed, you are a human being. You have the capacity to feel, hope, dream, think, strive, and aspire. Once you start taking classes, for that time in the classroom, you will be normal. You will feel just like every other college student in the country. You will learn, you will grow, you will have assignments and tests, you will have stresses and wins, and most of all, you will expand your mind and gain new perspectives about the world.

Education opens your mind to knowledge and grows you intellectually, mentally, and socially. The mind can become dormant, and like any other part of the human body, if you don't use it, you will lose you. Intellectual growth is one of the best gifts you can give yourself. Once you start learning, there is no limit on what you can learn and how much you can grow.

Education will put you in contact with people from the outside and grow your circle. You can never have too many people in your court. You may never know where these contacts will lead or how much you can grow as a result of these connections. You could gain a whole different perspective as chances are these people are not like you.

Education will provide an intellectual escape. Immersing yourself in content subjects, such as history, science, language, and math, will provide an intellectual escape for you and give you something to think about besides your current life. It will also give you something productive to occupy your time and keep you out of trouble. In addition to class time, you will likely have to work outside of the classroom to complete assignments, which can lead to a productive use of your time.

Writing for Reflection

- *Do you like to read? Why/why not?*

- *What kinds of materials would you be interested in reading?*

- *What kinds of reading material are currently available to you?*

- *Are there restrictions on what you are allowed to read?*

- *Do you have a source/person on the outside who can provide reading materials for you?*

- *What do you hope to gain out of reading?*

- *What are your reading goals? What resources are available to you?*

- *What is your current level of education?*

- *What are your thoughts on education?*

- *What educational programs are currently available to you?*

- *Are you making use of these programs? Why/why not?*

- *Do you want to receive a college degree? If so, what is stopping you from pursuing one?*

- *Have you taken advantage of the educational opportunities that have been offered to you? If not, why?*

- *Where can you go to find additional opportunities in your prison?*

- *Are you keeping a log of your reading? Set aside a part of your journal to be your "Reading Log". Label it and keep it up to date.*

Changing Your Narrative: Invest in Creativity

According to Google, creativity is the "use of our imaginations or original ideas, often in the production of artistic work." If we take this definition to heart, creativity does not just apply to those who embark on creative journeys to write novels or paint beautiful masterpieces. Many people have the misconception that if they do not have an artistic talent of some sort, there is no point in attempting creativity. This is not true. Every single person born alive has the ability to create, and it does not have to be mass produced or published to be impactful. In fact, I have written multiple short stories and three novels that I have no intention of publishing. For me, the act of creation is more important than the outcome.

The process of creation is more important than the product. We have often heard that the journey is more important than the destination. This is especially true about life. From the time we are born, our journey begins; we will arrive at our destination only when we take our last breath as a human being. If all of us were living solely for this destination—which is ultimately death for every single one of us—how sad would that be? Life is not about death; it is about the journey upon which we embark each and every day. It is a collection of those beautiful, painful, heartfelt, joyful, gut-wrenching single moments that we live each and every day. The older we get, the quicker those moments pass.

The same is true of our creative endeavors. While we all strive to complete something valuable and worthy in any artistic venture we begin, the process of creating that piece is just as important. The moments I spend writing are some of the most fulfilling of my life. I have heard the same about making music, painting or drawing, and producing videos. While I cannot deny that I experience a major sense of accomplishment when something in my mind finally makes it to some kind of tangible fruition, the process of getting there is equally as fulfilling. The act of creating gives me purpose and motivation.

We hunger for self-expression. To create means to grow. You may not feel this way, but most humans have a need for self-expression in their lives. Hence, why artistic works, such as songs, novels, movies, and paintings are so valuable to the human experience. These media—products of hours of labor and self-expression—bring us entertainment, joy, peace, and escape from the mundane day-to-day existence that most of us experience at one point another in our lives. Think about how boring and unfulfilling life would be without them. Think about how restricted you may feel being unable to see some of the movies or videos that you were able to view on the outside.

Each of these creative media has a story to tell. Self-expression and story-telling are at the heart of every creative process. Obviously written pieces tell stories, both fiction and non-fiction, that draw us into an author's world. Music is self-expression at its core, moving people in ways that other media cannot. Even an oil painting of a single scene is made to express the artist's mood or tell a story. When we think of famous people who are remembered long after their deaths, so many of them are artists and creators. Most of us have seen art by Leonardo da Vinci and Michelangelo. Again, think back to the previous lesson and the famous people I mentioned who have become immortalized by their creative works. Most of us have read works by Edgar Allan Poe and Stephen King. Most of us have heard music by Elvis Presley and Taylor Swift. Most of us have seen movies produced by George Lucas and Stephen Spielberg. Most of us have worked on computers with programs created by Steve Jobs and Bill Gates. What do all of these famous people have in common? These artists, writers, musicians, producers, and tech giants have all created some of the greatest artistic works of our time. Likely all of these endeavors began as a form of self-expression, a desire to make something bigger than themselves, or a means to tell a story.

Creative outlets can provide a healthy escape. One of the most popular artists of this era is singer/songwriter Taylor Swift. Whether we like her or hate her, no one can deny that she has the ability to draw people of all ages, races, genders, and cultures from all around the world together in one moment at one place in time to experience her music. People who attend her concerts often claim it is one of the greatest experiences of their lives, and the videos of massive crowds transfixed and swaying in complete unison while watching her on stage seem to support this. No matter what many of them are experiencing in their lives, her concerts and her music provide an escape from day-to-day life, from life's problems, from cancer, from failed relationships, and from everything in between.

Whether you are on the receiving end of creativity as in the case of a concert or the one creating, creative outlets have the ability to provide a healthy escape for what is going on around you. Writing novels provides an escape, as does reading them. Creating music provides an escape, as does listening to songs. If you want an escape from the dark place where prison may take you emotionally, skip the drugs and invest yourself in a creative outlet. You will be surprised both at what you will feel and what you may end up creating in the process. Even if you are not the most talented, the act of creating can still be impactful. Remember, it is about the process, not the product.

Another added benefit is that research has also demonstrated creative arts can be used by both the right and left hemispheres of the brain to help an individual confront stored trauma and then find ways to minimize its impact on their emotional state. Think about that, especially if you have been a victim of trauma.

Writing has been proven to have healing qualities. One of the most healing creative outlets to pursue is writing. It also requires next to nothing in regard to supplies or equipment; in fact, all you need are paper and pen. Best of all, writing does not require special skills or talent and can be meaningful, even if you deem yourself the most basic of writers. As we learned early in this course, writing to journal and process have the ability to provide tangible ways to cope with feelings and emotions that might otherwise be buried deep within you. Because writing is a left-hemisphere activity, it engages the left side of the brain and provides concrete, tangible ways of dealing with negative emotions brought about by trauma, anxiety, and depression.

Creativity connects us with others through the human experience. Whether we want to face it or not, we are not made to be on this planet alone. Sometimes, especially if we are not familiar with acceptable social skills, we may find it hard to connect with others. Creative works are one way that we can connect with others without having to participate in social interaction. Poetry, music, and written works all help us identify with what others are going through, thus helping us feel not so alone. In fact, creative works may provide sustenance for us in our darkest hours. Think about the times when you have experienced something painful in life and you hear a song that speaks exactly to what you are going through. Or you read a poem or a blog that helps you realize that you are not alone in what you are experiencing. This is the gift of creativity.

Arts-in-Prison Programs can help. If your prison offers an arts-in-prisons program, it would be a great idea to take full advantage of it, even if you do not consider yourself creative or artistic. If you have never taken a class on any of the arts in the past, do not be afraid to try something new. You may be surprised by a talent you didn't know you had. You might discover that you simply enjoy being creative. If you do not have access to such a program, you can still draw, paint, or write short stories in your free time. Remember, you do not have to possess what you might deem creative talent to use artistic works to better yourself.

Writing for Reflection

- *Do you consider yourself a creative person? Explain.*

- *Do you enjoy reading? If so, why? If not, why?*

- *Do you enjoy listening to music? If so, why? If not, why?*

- *Do you enjoy watching movies? If so, why? If not, why?*

- *Do you enjoy looking at art? If so, why? If not, why?*

- *Are there any artistic endeavors that you have pursued in the past (writing, art, etc.)? What were the results of those endeavors?*

- *Are there any art programs that are currently available to you?*

- *If you could pursue any form of art, what would you pursue? What is stopping you from pursuing that?*

- *What would you hope to gain out of the pursuit of an artistic endeavor?*

- *What would help you gain confidence to pursue an artistic endeavor?*

- *Describe any experiences in the past (movies, concerts, books, etc.) where you were so completely engaged and invested that you forgot all about the rest of your life.*

- *What do you see as the advantages of finding a creative outlet?*

- *What are the obstacles for you to pursue a creative outlet (i.e. money, supplies, etc.)?*

Changing Your Narrative: Change Your Mindset

Did you know that, on average, your brain will process between 60,000 and 70,000 thoughts per day? That is a lot of thinking! Given this, what we think about has a definite impact on other aspects of our lives, including our emotional state and our physical body. As we have discussed several times throughout this study, you cannot always control what happens outside of your mind, but you can control what goes on inside. You have control over your mindset. I have seen some people who have everything anyone could possibly want in life (money, success, a great family) and yet still be some of the most miserable people I know. On the contrary, I have seen some of the most content people facing the most horrific of life circumstances, including extreme poverty, terminal illness, and the loss of loved ones. Contentment is a mindset, and it is one that anyone can possess.

A lake of inner peace exists in all of us. While it may be hard to believe, the human psyche is made for peace; it craves peace. In fact, the inverse of peace—stress—can shorten our life by years, if not decades. Heart disease, diabetes, cancer, and a host of other diseases all have at their root stress and anxiety.

Granted, attaining that lake of peace is easier said than done, especially for those who face prison life every day. However, you can choose peace, even if you do not reside in a peaceful environment. You can refrain from involving yourself in social disputes. You can refrain from engaging in violence or rebellion that could land you in detention or segregation. You can refrain from talking about or to people that are not the best individuals to have in your circle. You can keep to yourself when possible and surround yourself with positive individuals when you have the opportunity. You can refrain from prison drama and focus on other outlets we have discussed so far in this writing study. So many aspects of your life are chosen for you, from the clothes you wear to the food you eat, to how long you get to be outside. You have so little control over your life the way it is, so why give up control over your thoughts too? You don't have to live in a prison in your mind, even if you have to live in one in your body. No one can take away your peace unless you allow it.

Positive thinking requires positive doing. You may have heard the phrase, "Fake it 'til you make it." While many disagree with this mantra, there is a bit of research to back up the truth of this statement. While most of the time, our actions follow our thoughts, sometimes the adverse can be true. Our actions can lead to a change in our thoughts. Hence, if you force yourself into a positive action, such as enrolling in classes, attending a drug rehab class, or joining a Bible study group, that decision may lead to a change in your thought patterns. You might even find yourself engaging in or enjoying those efforts. It is hard to be negative when you are sitting in front of people who are there for your betterment and who honestly want to see you succeed. Prison staff and especially prison volunteers typically take part in prison programs because they care about your well-being, and they want to invest in you.

If you want to improve your life, it takes more than intention. It takes action; it requires making the hard decisions and taking the hard steps. You may have also heard the phrase, "The road to hell is paved with good intentions." Intentions mean absolutely nothing. If I tell the loved one of a deceased friend that I "intended" to call her when she was alive, it means nothing. If I intend to lose weight but do not change my diet or fail to exercise, I will not lose weight. You can sit in your cell all day long and think about all the changes you intend to make in your life, but every single one of those thoughts mean nothing if you don't do something about it. You have to "do" to find the best version of you.

Choose the room of optimism. A good question to ask yourself as we come to the second to the last lesson of this program: in what "room" do you most often reside? Is it the angry room? The joyful room? The room of negativity? The room of optimism? There are some definite benefits to choosing the room of optimism. In addition to making you feel better emotionally, it also has various physical benefits. Being optimistic is good for your health, will build a stronger immune system, will help you live longer, and will help you produce the chemical that induces happiness—endorphins.

Develop a growth mindset. In addition to mindfulness, another popular term in the plethora of self-help books these days is growth mindset. What is this and what does it mean? If you are going to change anything about your life, you must embrace a growth mindset. This entails letting go of what you have always done and allowing yourself to try something new. It means looking at your life and situation from different perspectives and different angles. It means opening your mind to possibilities that you may not have otherwise considered.

To have a growth mindset, you need to stop making excuses and playing the blame game. Take responsibility for what has happened to you. Own your mistakes and take steps to prevent yourself from making these same mistakes in the future. As has been mentioned, it is common knowledge that many released convicts return to prison a second and third time, often for the same crimes. If you are lucky enough to get released and you find yourself back behind bars a second time, you have no one to blame but yourself. You knew what you were facing by continuing to live a life of crime. You were stuck in a fixed mindset and chose not to grow.

Strive for the better version of yourself. You do not have to settle for the you of your past. The you of the present is the most important person in your life. If you focus on this person and take the steps to be that person, you may find a better life in store for you. However, you must not be afraid to let go of your past and the you who landed yourself in prison in the first place.

Writing for Reflection

- *What or whom do you blame for your current imprisonment?*

- *What or whom do you blame for your current state of mind?*

- *How many times have you been incarcerated?*

- *If you came back a subsequent time after your initial stay in prison, why? What led you to return?*

- *What steps can you take to ensure that you will not return to prison again?*

- *What are some of the life tenants that you hold to be unchanging?*

- *What are some areas of life that you would be willing to change your mindset?*

- *Describe the best version of yourself.*

- *What qualities does this version of you possess?*

- *What does this person look like physically, mentally, emotionally?*

- *What steps can you take to become this person?*

Changing Your Narrative: Create Your Plan

Intent without action does not yield results. Hence, why this last lesson will focus on a concrete plan with tangible steps that you can take to explore the better versions of yourself.

Show up. The first thing you can do is the easiest part. Put one foot in front of the other. If you enroll in a class or program, show up. Don't make excuses as to why you cannot attend, even if you don't want to go. Even when you don't feel like it, even when you are tired, when you would rather veg out on your bunk and make the world go away, make the effort. Nothing worth doing is easy, or everyone would be living their best life. True change starts with what you do—your actions—and sometimes the hardest part is showing up.

Often when you take the first step and make yourself physically present, you will find it easier to become mentally present. You may learn something new or discover a new perspective or attitude. Taking a class, getting a certificate or degree, doing homework, studying—all of it takes discipline. Once you learn discipline, showing up will become second nature to you.

Be aware of your emotions and avoid reacting to what is going on around you. Think back to the rooms where you choose to live—the ones that will incur positive results. Resist the urge to go to the rooms where you will make bad decisions or engage in behavior that will land you in trouble and undo many of the positive changes you may be making in your life. Choose your reactions and emotions wisely, or you may find yourself more deeply imprisoned than you already are. Sometimes you might find yourself locked in these bad rooms with no way out.

Face and fight your addictions. If you have an addiction and there are resources to help you overcome it, you have to get help. This is easier said than done, even for those on the outside. However, if you remain a slave to any addiction, whether it be porn, drugs, alcohol, or even food, it is hard to focus on anything else. Most addicts have little control over their actions or decisions; rather, the source of the addiction becomes their god and is all consuming. Drug use is rampant in prisons, even in the most well-run institutions; drugs numb emotional pain and create an alternative reality, often allowing offenders to avoid dealing with the ramifications of their crimes. It also makes them easier to control for prison personnel. Don't become a prisoner to drugs as well. They may make you feel good in the short term, but such a feeling is fleeting and temporary. In reality, they are destroying your body, your brain cells, and your life. You know this. You will not be able to make any progress toward any goal if you have an addiction. It will get in the way of an education, a job, and even relationships. Addiction is the Terminator of the better version of you.

Invest in other people. While it feels like life is all about us, it really isn't. If it were, we would all be born on our own deserted islands with no one around and no one to bother us. We would not need other humans to create life. Being solo in this world, while it may be the easiest and the least painful, is not the most rewarding. Think about all the best moments of your life to date. Do you have any good memories? Of prior loves? Of family times? Of children being born? Of vacations? Of successful achievements? Chances are pretty good that most of these good memories probably included other people. It is hard to deny that we were made to be with others. We were not biologically or emotionally made to be alone in this world, even if some of you feel like you are.

This is why you can never go wrong by investing in other people. There is always someone out there in this world who is worse off than you are, even if you don't feel like it. Often when we focus on others, it is easier to forget our own woes. Sometimes, even doing so helps us put our own issues into perspective. In the process, too, we might discover gifts and talents we had no idea we possessed, and we might just make someone's life a little bit better.

Create your long-term vision or life mission statement. Write it down. Now is the time to form the mental image of the better version of you. What does that person look like?

What qualities does that person have? What is the vision for your life, both in and out-side of prison? What is the mission statement that will guide you as you move forward? Again, this goes back to your why. What is your purpose in the time you have left on this planet?

This vision needs to be tangible; having it floating around in your head won't do. Once you write it down, put it in a place where you can read it and be reminded of what you can become. You have probably heard the statement, "If you fail to plan, you plan to fail." This statement is also true of your life's mission. If you don't have a mission or vision, then it will be hard to make a plan. The vision will guide your plan, your systems, and your goals, and act as the umbrella statement for everything you do from now on.

Establish your goals, and identify tasks for those goals. Write them down. Once you have your vision, it is time to form your goals, both short term and long term. What are these goals? They could be goals that relate to your health, a job, relationships, your education, your mental health, your finances, hobbies, creative endeavors, and other aspects of your life. You can categorize them.

Once you have the goals, you need to write down concrete action steps or a list of tasks that you must do to complete these goals. For example, if you want to get a college degree, your tasks might include: apply for a program, enroll and choose your classes, go to class, do your assignments, read your homework, study for tests, and complete all the requirements requested by the instructor. If you want to start exercising, your tasks might include: research to find a fitness program, decide on what exercises you are going to do, set up an exercise schedule, exercise on the days you select, and record your progress.

Make small changes and take small steps to create big changes. One of the reasons that many people fail at meeting goals they set for themselves is that they take on too much at once and set their expectations way too high. This might look like: I am going to lose 30 pounds, so I am giving up sugar, exercising 30 minutes every day, drinking eight glasses of water daily, and going on a diet. If these action steps were not implemented slowly and had not already become habits, chances are slim that I will be able to accomplish all of these things at once. I may have a successful one or two weeks, but is this truly sustainable if I am not a very disciplined person?

Any change you make in your life must be sustainable, which means you need to be able to do it for the long haul. The best way to do this, according to many therapists, is to implement one small change at a time and focus on that one change until it becomes a part of your routine. Then when you have mastered that goal, move on to the next. This will be beneficial for several reasons. For one, being able to complete one task at a time will be more doable; it will also bolster your confidence. It will show you that you are capable of accomplishing goals—and of positive change in your life.

Finally, it will allow you to move on to the next goal and put your focus on that. If tasks that are put into place to accomplish your goals become routine, a time will come when you won't even have to think about it; you will just get up and do it, and you won't need to expend any mental energy toward it.

Creating small positive changes will eventually lead to success in big ways. For example, if you are on a weight loss journey, and you lose one pound a week, in five months, you will have lost 20 pounds, and have probably been able to keep it off. If you are going for a college degree, and you focus on your courses that you are taking one semester at a time, you will be finished with a degree in two to four years, depending on the program.

If possible, purchase a calendar or planner on which you can record your vision statement, your goals, and your day-to-day "to do" tasks. Or have a friend or family member do so. Keep this in a safe place and consult it daily. Record your thoughts and emotions on each given day; tell whether you were able to accomplish the daily tasks that you set out to do.

When we think about change, it is easy to get caught up in what you need to do to become the better version of yourself overnight, but that seldom works. You have to start with one goal at a time. This way, you will not feel overwhelmed or overburdened, and you will most likely be able to make the change you need.

Writing for Reflection

- *What is your approach when you have something that you don't want to do, but you know you need to do it anyway?*

- *What steps can you take to show up—even when you don't feel like it?*

- *What are your triggers that put you in the emotional rooms that cause you pain?*

- *What steps can you take to avoid these triggers?*

- *What are some changes you can make to take better control of your emotions?*

- *Do you have an addiction? If so, what is it?*

- *Have you had an addiction in the past? If so, what was it?*

- *Have you taken steps in the past to overcome this addiction? If so, what have you done?*

- *What was the result of this intervention?*

- *What is the current state of your addiction?*

- *Are there resources currently available to help you overcome this addiction? Are you utilizing these resources? If so, what is the result? If not, why not?*

- *Write down your long-term vision or mission statement.*

- *Make a list of your short-term goals (within the next six months to a year).*

- *Make a list of your long-term goals (within the next five years).*

- *Make a list of the tasks/small steps that you need to do to accomplish each goal.*

Wrapping Up

As we conclude this writing journey, I hope you were able to discover ways that you can become the better version of you. You were not made to be a miserable, destructive human being, even if you feel like that. Remember, our thoughts and feelings are not reality, and even if we do not have control over external aspects of our life, we can control our internal self—all those pieces of us that make up our spirit, our intellect, and our soul.

You were not made to waste away in a cell, to obliterate your mind with drugs, and to spend your days aimlessly trying to survive. You were made for better. Now act like it! Go out there and be the best version of you that you can become.